Something Is Strange about Paula's New Friends

ST NICHOLAS HOUSE
Bunkers Lane
Hemel Hempstead
Hertfordshire
HP3 8RP

Written by Billy Aronson ■ Illustrated by Joe Boddy

MODERN CURRICULUM PRESS

PROJECT DIRECTOR: Susan Cornell Poskanzer
ART DIRECTOR: Lisa Olsson

MODERN CURRICULUM PRESS, Imprint of Pearson Learning

299 Jefferson Road, Parsippany, NJ 07054
(800) 321-3106 / www.mcschool.com

This edition is published simultaneously in Canada by
Globe/Modern Curriculum Press, Toronto.

ISBN 0-8136-1156-3 (STY PK)   ISBN 0-8136-1157-1 (BB)   ISBN 0-8136-1158-X (SB)

10 9 8   02 01 00 99

One morning when Paula reached into her drawer,
she found it was filled with a huge **STEGOSAUR!**
She pulled on his foot till he came tumbling out.
Her socks were all stuck to his dinosaur snout.

She said, "You can't stay here, you big stegosaur!
You'll shatter the windows and batter the door!
So let's go outside, and we'll have lots of fun!
Just put on this hat to be safe in the sun."

They put on their hats and some sunglasses, too,
and went outside looking for something to do.
They jumped in a pool to get cool. It was fun!
Her friend swam so fast. He was second to none.

A lifeguard who saw them sat up in his seat.
"Maybe I've spent too much time in the heat.
But I think you will see in the pool at this end...
that something is strange
about Paula's new friend!"

Walking out of the pool, she said, "Wait just a minute.
I think that bush has
TRICERATOPS in it!"
Triceratops smiled. He loved what they wore.
So they bought him a hat of his own at the store.

The three of them went for a walk down the street.
Everyone stared and said,

        "Gosh!" "Gee!" and "Neat!"

As the new kids in town looked in shop after shop,
people started to gather; traffic came to a stop.

Then in the distance two skyscrapers shook.
Triceratops covered his eyes; he couldn't look.
Stegosaur pointed ahead with his claw
Out jumped two huge…

Can you guess what they saw?

"Why, sure!" Paula said. "But let's go to the store.
You two need some hats; I just hope they have more."
They skipped
        and they shopped
        all the way
            down the block.
All the people they passed looked a little in shock.

"I don't mean to stare," muttered Officer Izzard,
"but those kids have scales very much like a lizard.
As their toes hit the pavement, by golly, it bends!
Something is strange
about Paula's new friends!"

A music store window then caught her friends' eyes.
They wanted to try some guitars on for size!
So in marched the five of them, fast as they could.
A crowd formed around them; they sounded so good!

"Check out that forty foot jaw!" yelled one man.

"What a sharp look! What great claws!" roared a fan.

"These kids!" someone cried. "They can sure play guitars. Someday they're going to be very big stars!"

14

After they finished, they waved with their feet.
The audience thought that the band was so neat.
Even the store owner gave them a hand,
saying, "Something is cool
           about Paula's new band!"

Paula climbed home up a dinosaur stair.
Her friends scooted off in the fresh summer air.
And she thought to herself as she waved,
    "That was fine.
        But they sure were different,
            those new friends of mine!"